AF201092

Impressum
Verlag: BABADADA GmbH, Nedderfeld 112 , 22529 Hamburg
Geschäftsführer / Verlagsleitung: Harald Hof
Druck: Books on Demand GmbH, In de Tarpen 42, 22848 Norderstedt

Imprint
Publisher: BABADADA GmbH, Nedderfeld 112 , 22529 Hamburg, Germany
Managing Director / Publishing direction: Harald Hof
Print: Books on Demand GmbH, In de Tarpen 42, 22848 Norderstedt

school

escuela

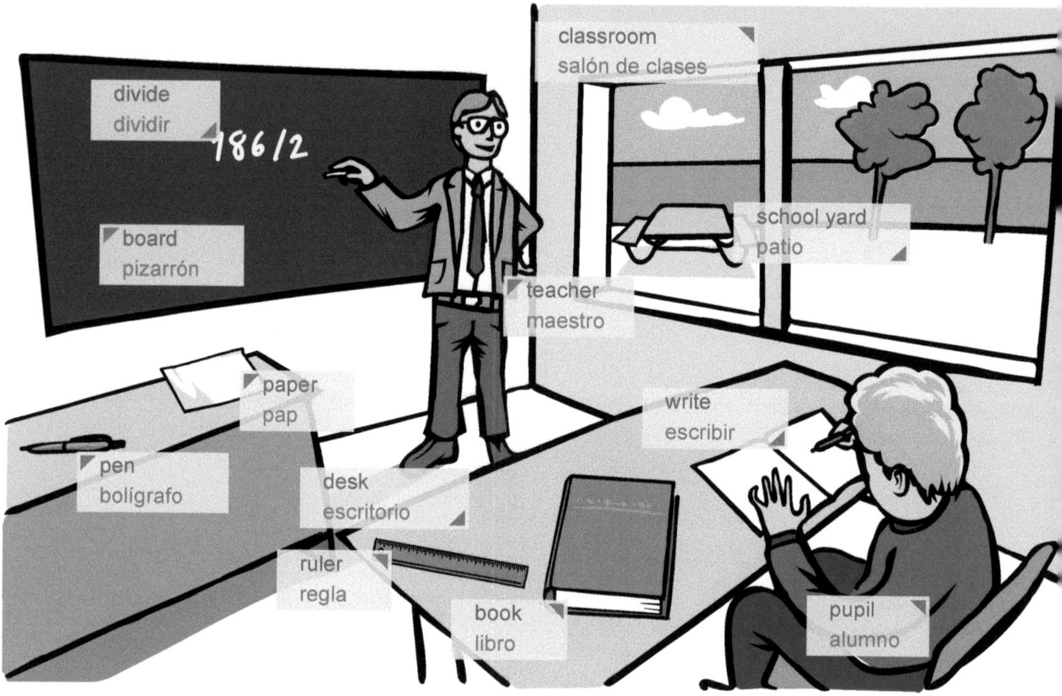

classroom
salón de clases
divide
dividir
186/2
board
pizarrón
school yard
patio
teacher
maestro
paper
pap
write
escribir
pen
bolígrafo
desk
escritorio
ruler
regla
book
libro
pupil
alumno

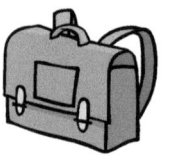

satchel

mochila

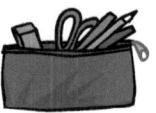

pencil case

caja de lápices

pencil

lápiz

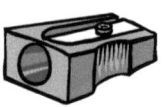

pencil sharpener

sacapuntas

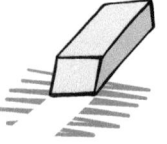

rubber

goma de borrar

drawing pad

bloc de dibujo

drawing

dibujo

paintbrush

pincel

paint box

caja de lápices de color

scissors

tijeras

glue

pegamento

exercise book

libro de ejercicios

homework

tarea

number

número

add

sumar

subtract

restar

multiply

multiplicar

calculate

calcular

letter

letra

alphabet

alfabeto

word

palabra

text
texto

read
leer

chalk
tiza

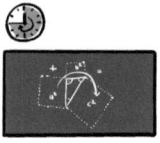

lesson
lección

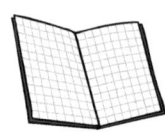

register
cuaderno de clase

examination
examen

certificate
certificado

school uniform
uniforme

education
educación

encyclopedia
enciclopedia

university
universidad

microscope
microscopio

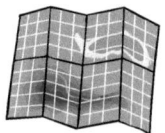

map
mapa

waste-paper basket
bote de basura

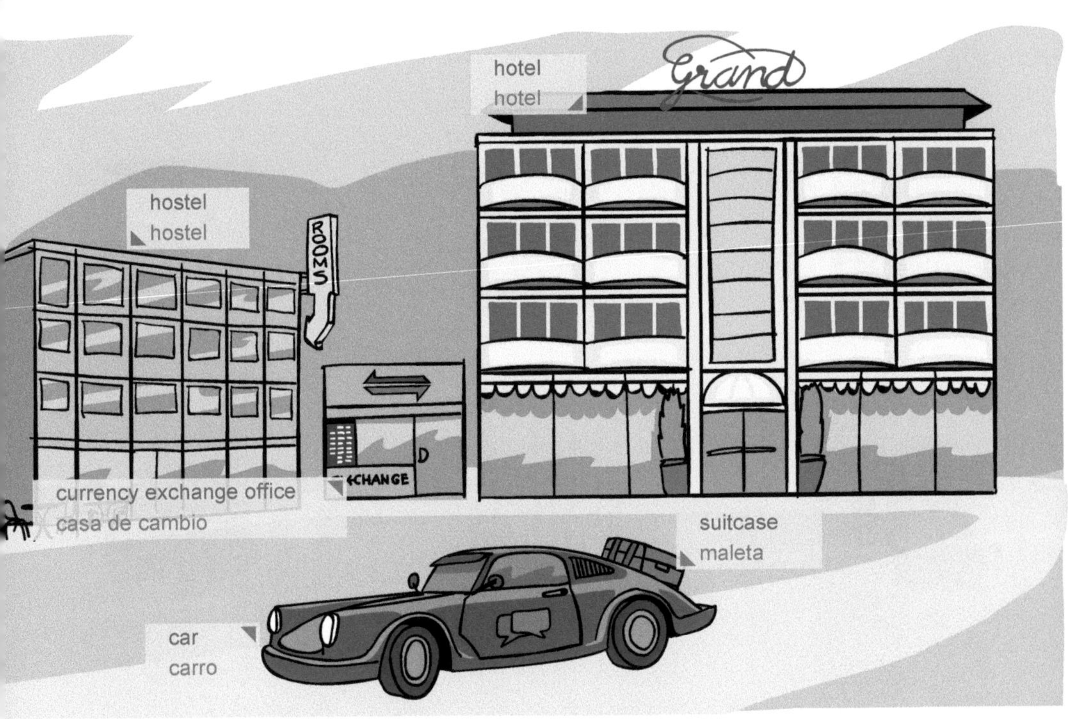
hotel
hotel
Grand
hostel
hostel
ROOMS
EXCHANGE
currency exchange office
casa de cambio
suitcase
maleta
car
carro

language

idioma

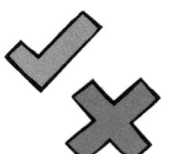

yes / no

sí / no

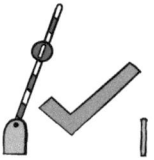

Okay

Órale

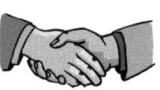

hello

hola

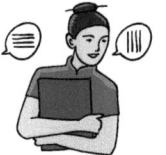

translator

traductor

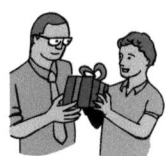

Thank you

Gracias

how much is...?

¿cuánto cuesta...?

I don´t get it

No entiendo

problem

problema

Good evening!

¡Buenas tardes!

Good morning!

¡Buenos días!

Good night!

¡Buenas noches!

goodbye

adiós

direction

dirección

luggage

equipaje

bag

bolsa

backpack

mochila

guest

invitado

room

recámara

sleeping bag

bolsa de dormir

tent

tienda de campaña

travel - viaje

tourist information

información turística

beach

playa

credit card

tarjeta de crédito

breakfast

desayuno

lunch

almuerzo

dinner

cena

Ticket

billete

elevator

ascensor

stamp

sello

border

frontera

customs

aduana

embassy

embajada

visa

visa

passport

pasaporte

transport
transporte

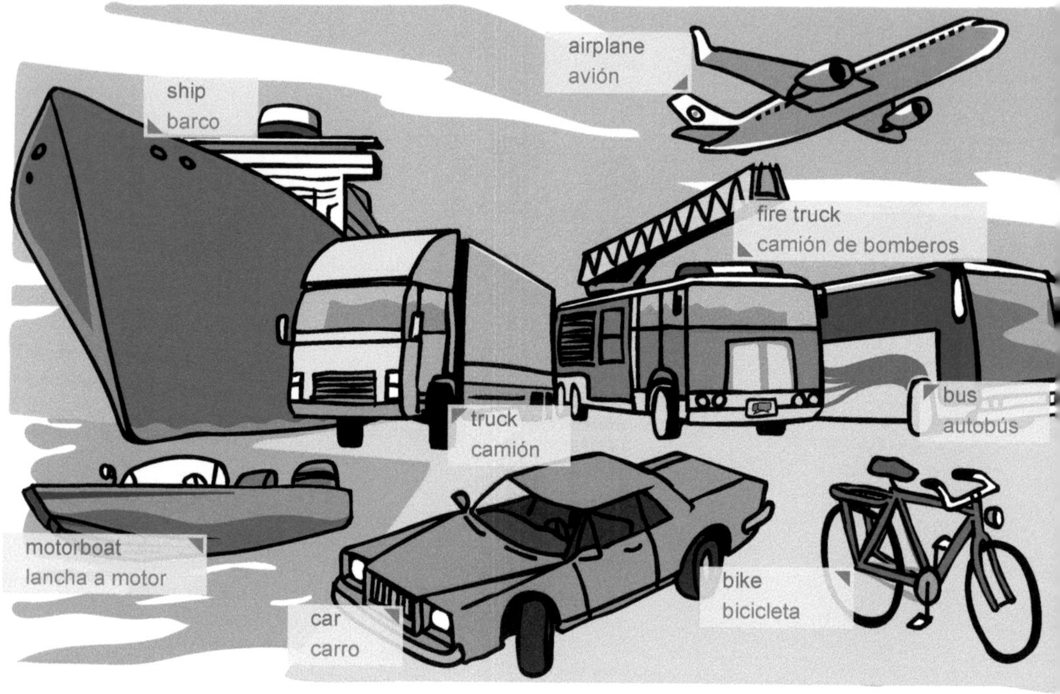

airplane
avión
ship
barco
fire truck
camión de bomberos
bus
autobús
truck
camión
motorboat
lancha a motor
bike
bicicleta
car
carro

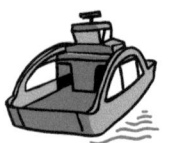

ferry

ferry

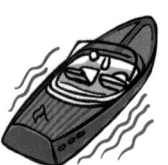

boat

bote

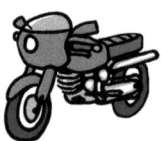

motorbike

motocicleta

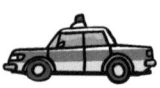

police car

patrulla

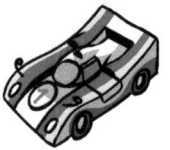

racing car

coche de carreras

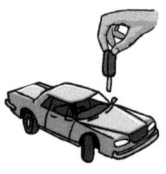

rental car

auto para rentar

car sharing

renta de autos

tow truck

grúa

garbage truck

camión recolector de basura

engine

motor

fuel

gasolina

fuel station

gasolinera

traffic sign

señal de tráfico

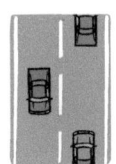

traffic

tránsito

traffic jam

embotellamiento

parking lot

aparcamiento

train station

estación de tren

tracks

vías

train

tren

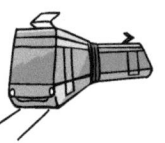

tram

tranvía

wagon

vagón

helicopter

helicóptero

airport

aeropuerto

tower

torre

passenger

pasajero

container

contenedor

carton

caja de cartón

cart

carretilla

basket

cesta

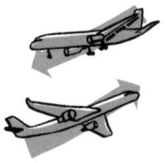

take off / land

despegar / aterrizar

city

ciudad

village

pueblo

city center

centro de ciudad

house

casa

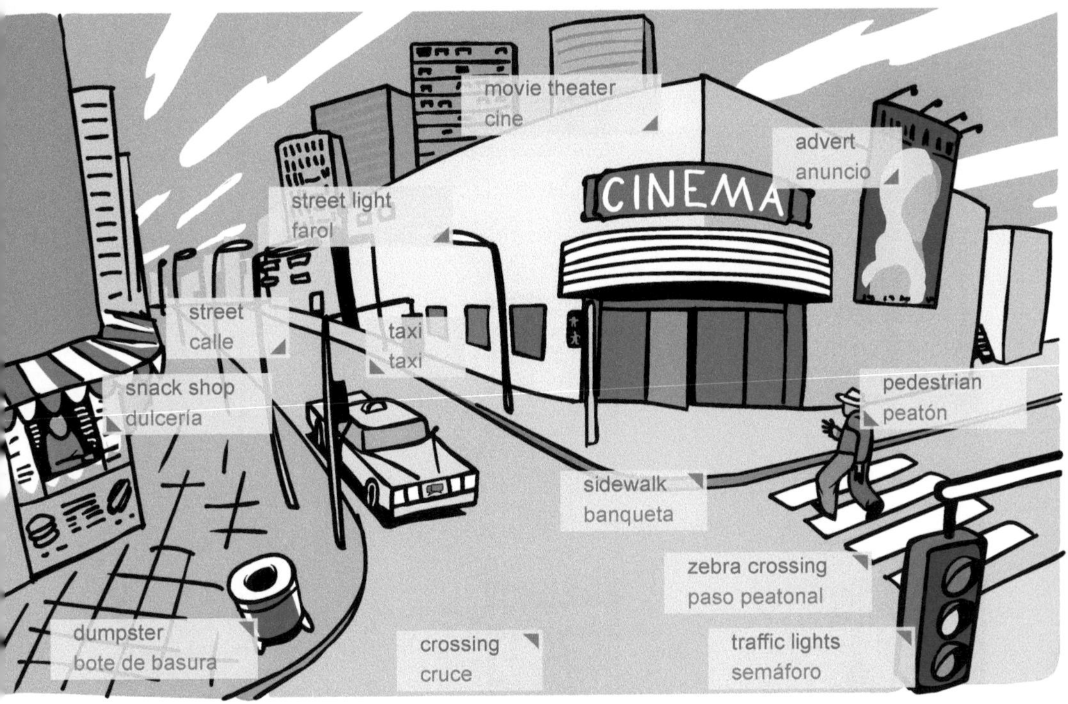

movie theater / cine

advert / anuncio

CINEMA

street light / farol

street / calle

taxi / taxi

pedestrian / peatón

snack shop / dulcería

sidewalk / banqueta

zebra crossing / paso peatonal

dumpster / bote de basura

crossing / cruce

traffic lights / semáforo

hut
cabaña

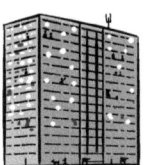

apartment
apartamento

train station
estación de tren

city hall
ayuntamiento

museum
museo

school
escuela

university

universidad

bank

banco

hospital

hospital

hotel

hotel

pharmacy

farmacia

office

oficina

book shop

librería

shop

tienda

flower shop

florería

supermarket

supermercado

market

mercado

department store

grandes tiendas

fishmonger's shop

pescadería

mall

centro comercial

harbor

puerto

park

parque

bench

banco

bridge

puente

stairs

escaleras

subway

metro

tunnel

túnel

bus stop

parada de autobús

bar

bar

restaurant

restaurante

postbox

buzón

street sign

letrero

parking meter

parquímetro

zoo

zoológico

swimming pool

alberca

mosque

mezquita

city - ciudad

farm
granja

pollution
contaminación

cemetery
cementerio

church
iglesia

playground
área de niños

temple
templo

landscape

paisaje

leaf
hoja

signpost
señal

path
camino

meadow
pradera

stone
piedra

tree
árbol

hiker
caminante

river
río

grass
pasto

flower
flor

valley

valle

hill

montaña

lake

lago

forest

bosque

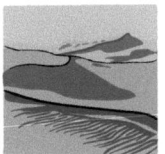

desert

desierto

volcano

volcán

castle

castillo

rainbow

arco iris

mushroom

champiñón

palm tree

palmera

mosquito

mosquito

fly

mosca

ant

hormiga

bee

abeja

spider

araña

landscape - paisaje

beetle

escarabajo

frog

rana

squirrel

ardilla

hedgehog

erizo

hare

liebre

owl

lechuza

bird

pájaro

swan

cisne

boar

jabalí

deer

ciervo

moose

alce

dam

embalse

wind turbine

turbina eólica

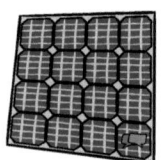

solar panel

pansolar

climate

clima

restaurant
restaurante

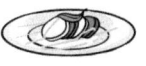

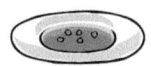

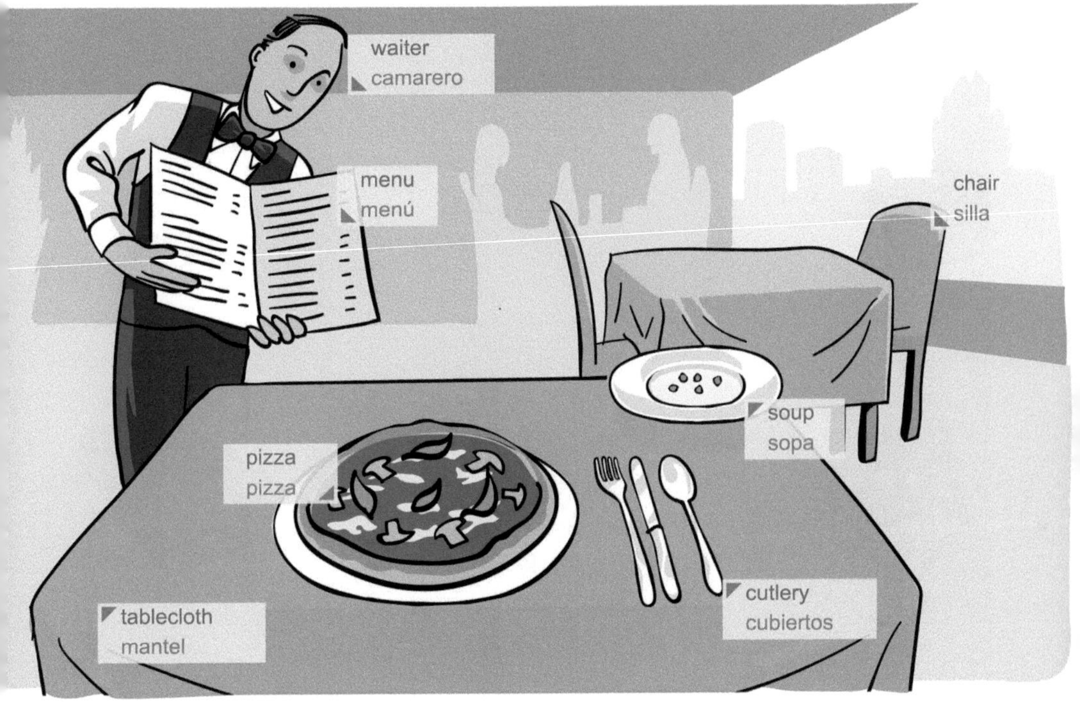
waiter
camarero
menu
menú
chair
silla
soup
sopa
pizza
pizza
cutlery
cubiertos
tablecloth
mantel

starter

entrada

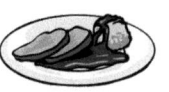

main course

plato fuerte

dessert

postre

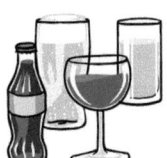

drinks

bebidas

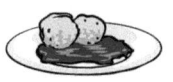

food

comida

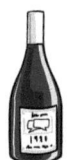

bottle

botella

fast food

comida rápida

street food

comida de calle

teapot

tetera

sugar bowl

azucarera

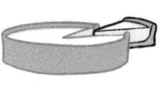

portion

porción

espresso machine

cafetera espresso

high chair

periquera

bill

cuenta

tray

charola

knife

cuchillo

fork

tenedor

spoon

cuchara

teaspoon

cuchara de té

serviette

servilleta

glass

vaso

restaurant - restaurante

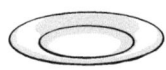

plate
plato

soup plate
plato hondo

saucer
plato

sauce
salsa

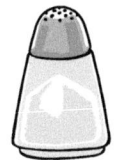

salt shaker
salero

pepper mill
molino para pimienta

vinegar
vinagre

oil
aceite

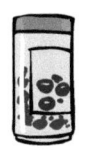 

spices
especias

ketchup
kétchup

mustard
mostaza

mayonnaise
mayonesa

supermarket
supermercado

special offer
oferta especial
FOR
customer
cliente
dairy products
productos lácteos
fruit
fruta
shopping cart
carrito para compras

BUTCHERS

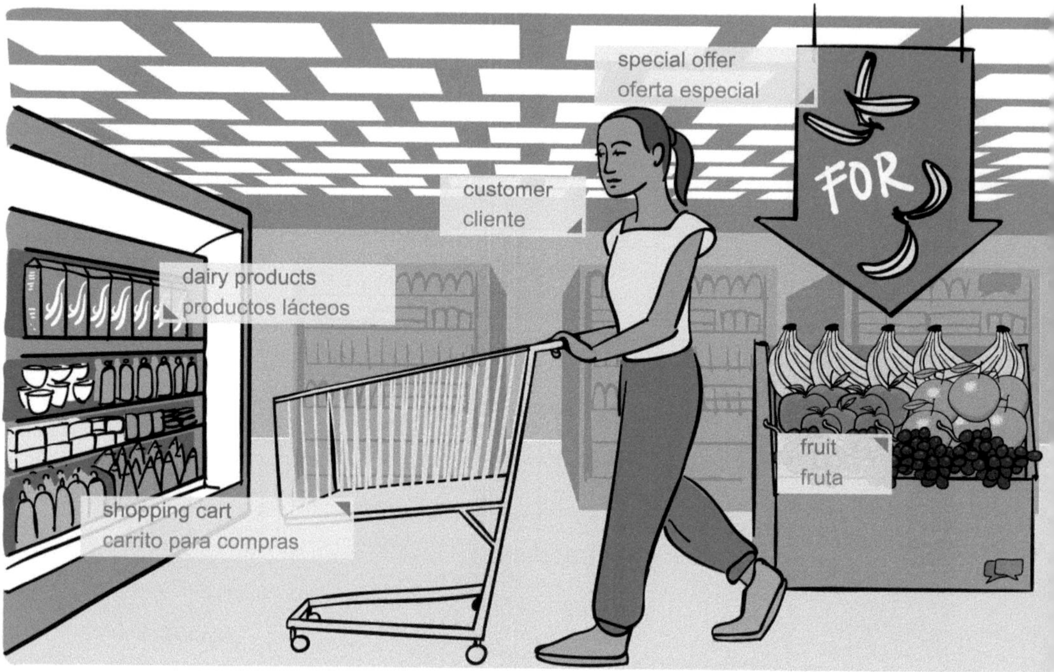

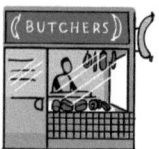

butcher's shop

carnicería

BAKERY

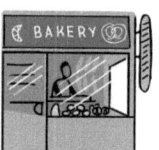

bakery

panadería

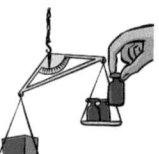

weigh

pesar

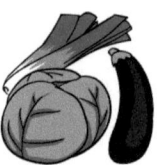

vegetables

vegetales

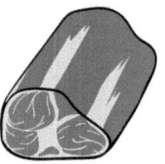

meat

carne

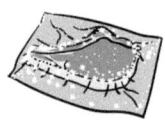

frozen food

alimentos congelados

cold cuts
carnes frías

canned food
alimentos enlatados

detergent
detergente en polvo

candy
dulces

household products
electrodomésticos

cleaning products
productos de limpieza

sales representative
vendedora

cash register
caja

cashier
cajero

shopping list
lista de compras

opening hours
horario de atención al público

wallet
cartera

credit card
tarjeta de crédito

bag
bolsa

plastic bag
bolsa de plástico

water
....
agua

juice
....
jugo

milk
....
leche

coke
....
refresco de cola

wine
....
vino

beer
....
cerveza

alcohol
....
alcohol

cocoa
....
cacao

tea
....
té

coffee
....
café

espresso
....
espresso

cappuccino
....
cappuccino

banana

plátano

apple

manzana

orange

naranja

melon

melón

lemon

limón

carrot

zanahoria

garlic

ajo

bamboo

bambú

onion

cebolla

mushroom

champiñón

nuts

nueces

noodles

fideos

spaghetti

espaguetis

rice

arroz

salad

ensalada

fries

patatas fritas

fried potatoes

patatas fritas

pizza

pizza

hamburger

hamburguesa

sandwich

emparedado

escalope

filete

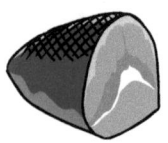

ham

jamón

salami

salami

sausage

salchicha

chicken

pollo

roast

asado

fish

pescado

porridge oats

copos de avena

muesli

muesli

cornflakes

copos de maíz

flour

harina

croissant

cuernito

bread roll

bolillo

bread

pan

toast

tostada

cookies

galletas

butter

mantequilla

curd

cuajada

cake

pastel

egg

huevo

fried egg

huevo frito

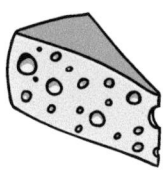

cheese

queso

ice cream

helado

sugar

azúcar

honey

miel

jelly

mermelada

nougat cream

crema de chocolate

curry

curry

farm
granja

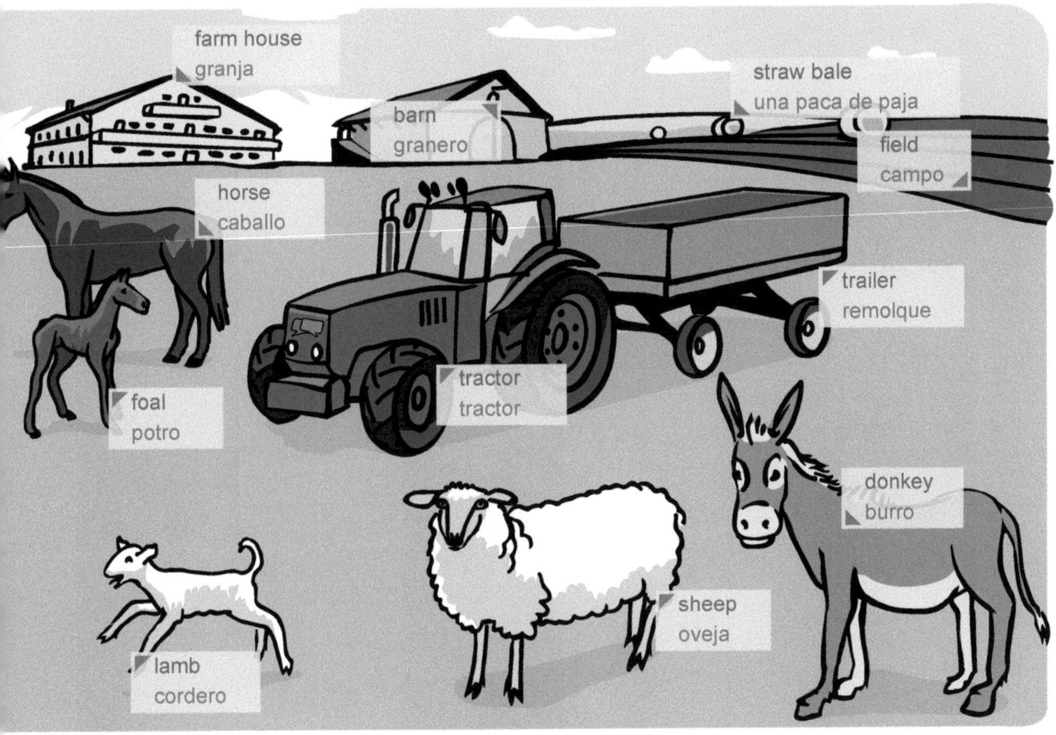
farm house
granja
barn
granero
straw bale
una paca de paja
field
campo
horse
caballo
trailer
remolque
tractor
tractor
foal
potro
donkey
burro
sheep
oveja
lamb
cordero

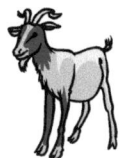

goat

cabra

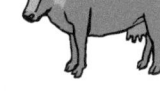

cow

vaca

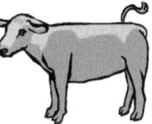

calf

ternero

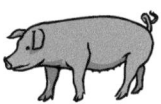

pig

cerdo

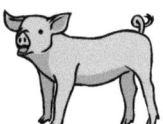

piglet

lechón

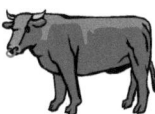

bull

toro

goose

ganso

duck

pato

chick

pollo

hen

gallina

cockerel

gallo

rat

rata

cat

gato

mouse

ratón

ox

buey

dog

perro

dog house

casa dperro

garden hose

manguera

watering can

regadera

scythe

guadaña

plow

arado

sickle

hoz

hoe

azadón

pitchfork

horquilla

axe

hacha

pushcart

carretilla

trough

bebedero

milk can

bote de leche

sack

saco

fence

valla

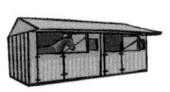

stable

establo

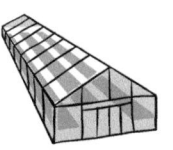

greenhouse

invernadero

soil

suelo

seed

semilla

fertilizer

fertilizador

combine harvester

cosechadora

harvest

cosechar

harvest

cosecha

yams

camote

wheat

trigo

soya

soja

potato

patata

corn

maíz

rapeseed

semilde colza

fruit tree

árbol frutal

manioc

mandioca

grain

cereales

house
casa

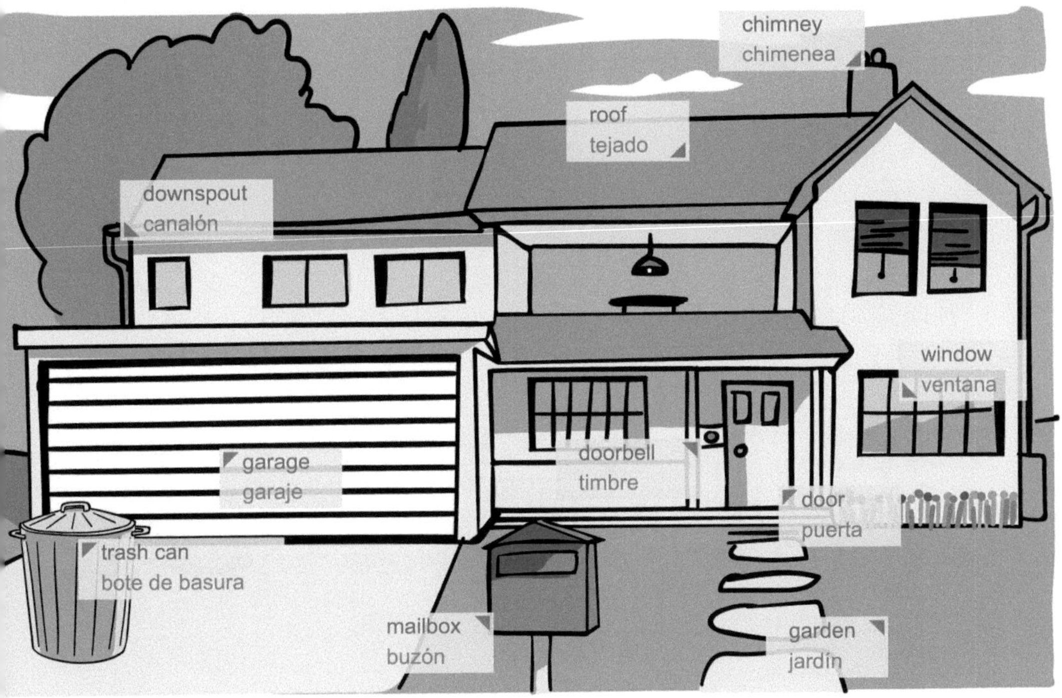
chimney
chimenea
roof
tejado
downspout
canalón
window
ventana
garage
garaje
doorbell
timbre
door
puerta
trash can
bote de basura
mailbox
buzón
garden
jardín

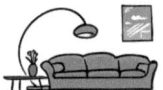

living room
estancia

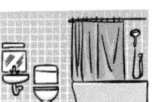

bathroom
baño

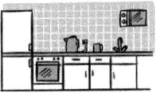

kitchen
cocina

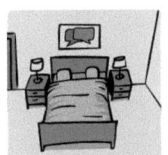

bedroom
recámara

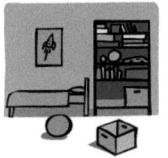

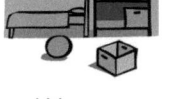

kids room
recámara de los niños

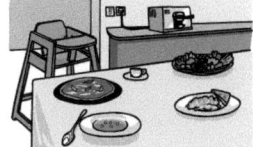

dining room
comedor

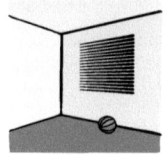

floor

suelo

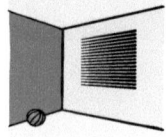

wall

pared

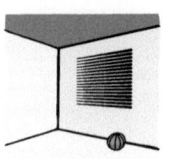

ceiling

techo

cellar

sótano

sauna

sauna

balcony

balcón

terrace

terraza

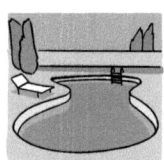

pool

alberca

lawn mower

cortacésped

sheet

sábana

bedspread

colcha

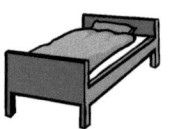

bed

cama

broom

escoba

bucket

balde

switch

interruptor

living room
estancia

wallpaper
pappara empapelar
picture
imagen
lamp
lámpara
shelf
estante
cabinet
alacena
television
televisión
fireplace
chimenea
flower
flor
cushion
cojín
sofa
sofá
vase
florero
remote control
control remoto

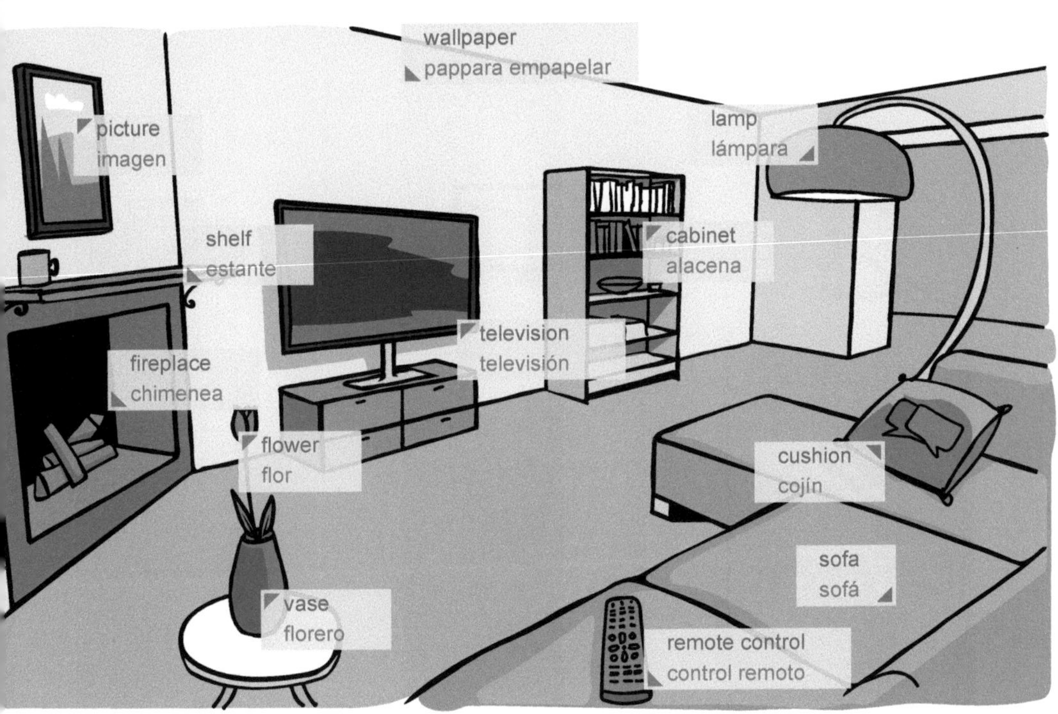

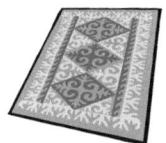

carpet

alfombra

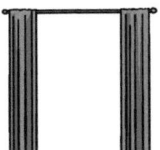

drape

cortina

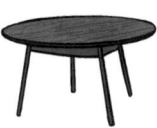

table

mesa

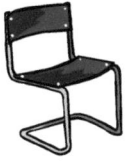

chair

silla

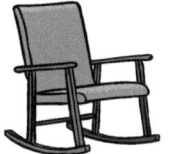

rocking chair

mecedora

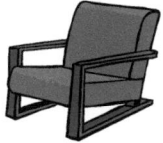

armchair

sillón

book

libro

blanket

frazada

decoration

decoración

firewood

leña

film

película

stereo system

equipo de música

key

llave

newspaper

periódico

painting

pintura

poster

póster

radio

radio

notebook

cuaderno

vacuum cleaner

aspiradora

cactus

cactus

candle

vela

kitchen

cocina

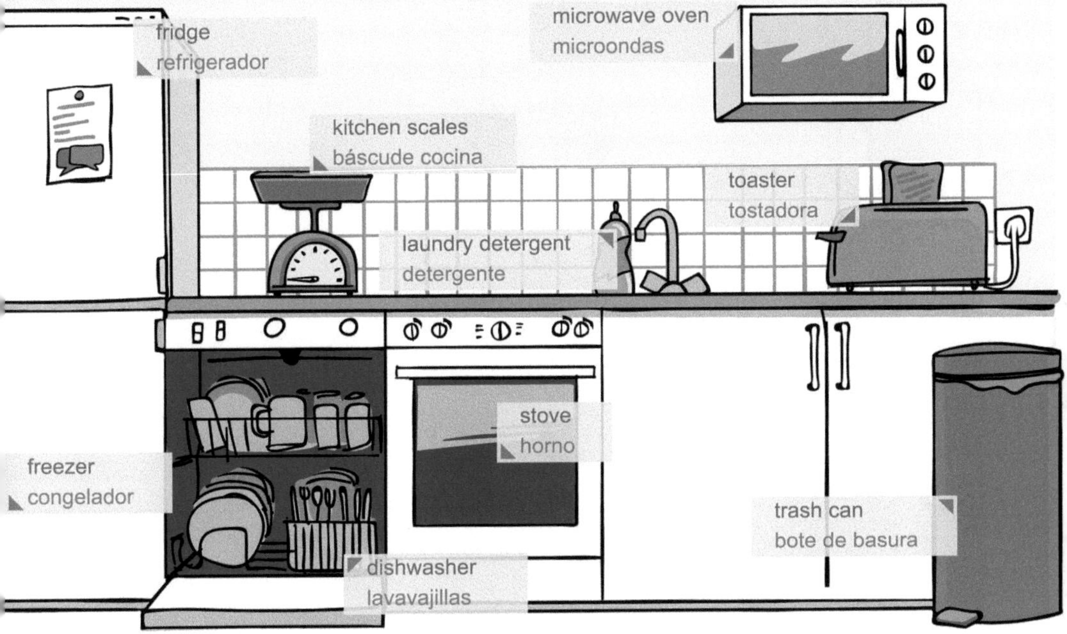
fridge
refrigerador
microwave oven
microondas
kitchen scales
báscude cocina
toaster
tostadora
laundry detergent
detergente
stove
horno
freezer
congelador
trash can
bote de basura
dishwasher
lavavajillas

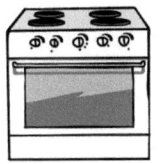

cooker

opresión

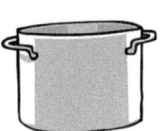

pot

olla

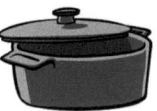

cast-iron pot

olde hierro fundido

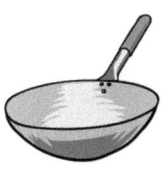

wok / kadai

wok

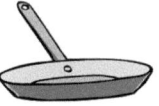

pan

sartén

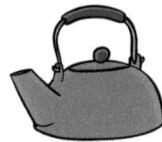

kettle

hervidor

steamer

vaporera

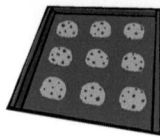

baking tray

charode horno

crockery

loza

mug

taza

bowl

bol

chopsticks

palillos

ladle

cucharón

spatula

espátula

whisk

batidora

strainer

colador

sieve

colador

grater

rallador

mortar

mortero

barbecue

barbacoa

fireplace

fogata

chopping board

tabpara picar

rolling pin

rodillo para amasar

corkscrew

sacacorchos

can

lata

can opener

abrelatas

oven cloth

guante de cocina

sink

fregadero

brush

cepillo

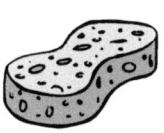

sponge

esponja

blender

batidora

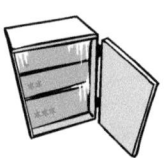

deep freezer

congelador

baby bottle

biberón

tap

llave

kitchen - cocina

bathroom
baño

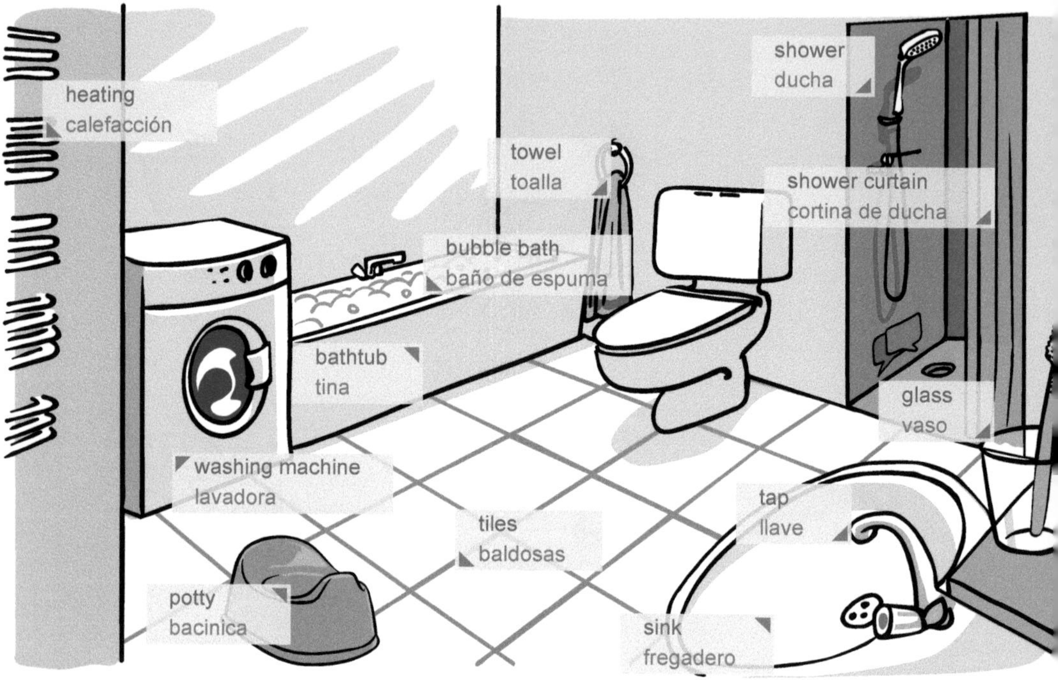

heating
calefacción
towel
toalla
shower
ducha
shower curtain
cortina de ducha
bubble bath
baño de espuma
bathtub
tina
glass
vaso
washing machine
lavadora
tap
llave
tiles
baldosas
potty
bacinica
sink
fregadero

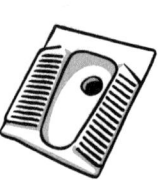

toilet

inodoro

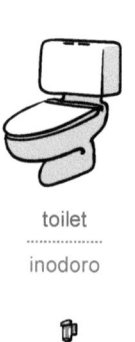

squat toilet

letrina

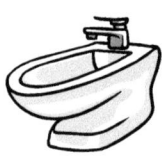

bidet

bidé

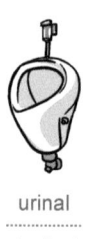

urinal

mingitorio

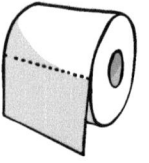

toilet paper

paphigiénico

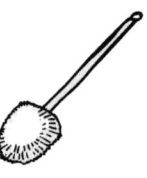

toilet brush

cepillo para baño

toothbrush

cepillo de dientes

toothpaste

pasta dental

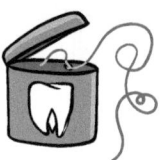

dental floss

hilo dental

wash

lavar

hand shower

ducha de mano

douche

ducha vaginal

basin

fregadero

back brush

cepillo de espalda

soap

jabón

shower gel

gde ducha

shampoo

champú

flannel

toallita

drain

drenaje

creme

crema

deodorant

desodorante

mirror

espejo

hand mirror

espejo de tocador

razor

máquina para afeitar

shaving foam

espuma de afeitar

aftershave

loción para después de
afeitar

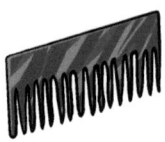

comb

peine

brush

cepillo

hair-dryer

secadora

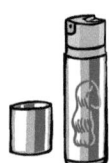

hairspray

laca

makeup

maquillaje

lipstick

lápiz labial

nail varnish

esmalte para uñas

cotton wool

algodón

nail scissors

tijeras para uñas

perfume

perfume

washbag

estuche para cosméticos

stool

taburete

weighing scales

báscula

bathrobe

bata

rubber gloves

guantes de goma

tampon

tampón

sanitary towel

toalsanitaria

chemical toilet

baño móvil

kids room
recámara de los niños

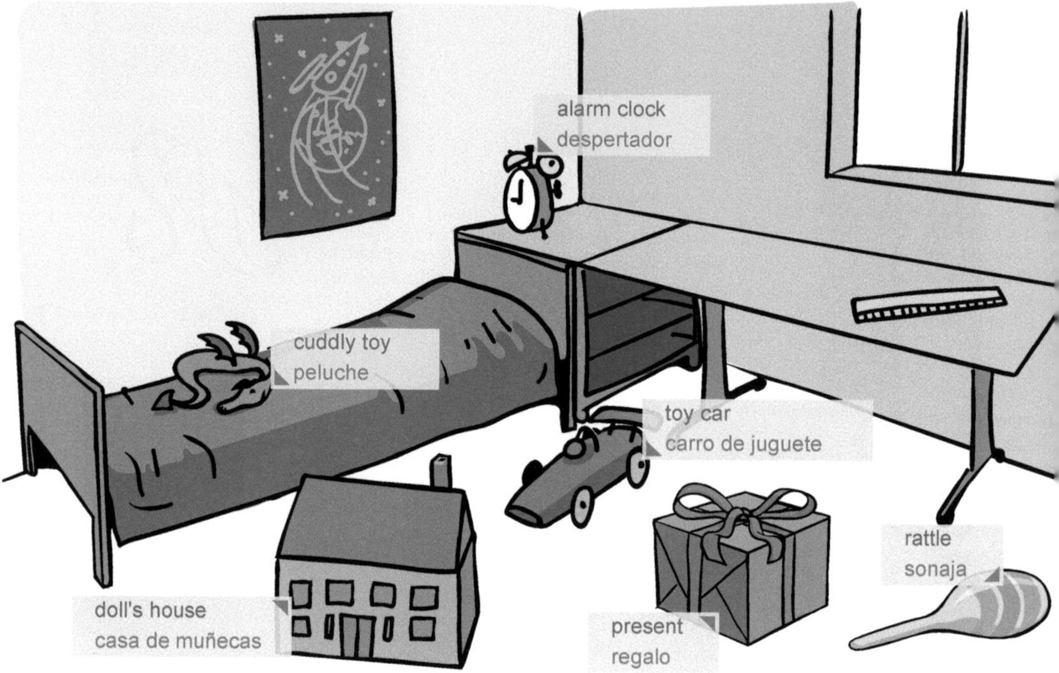

alarm clock
despertador

cuddly toy
peluche

toy car
carro de juguete

rattle
sonaja

doll's house
casa de muñecas

present
regalo

balloon

globo

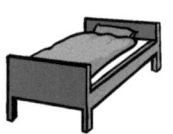

bed

cama

stroller

carriola

deck of cards

cartas

jigsaw

rompecabezas

comic

cómic

lego bricks

piezas de lego

toy blocks

bloques para jugar

action figure

figura de acción

romper suit

mameluco

frisbee

frisbee

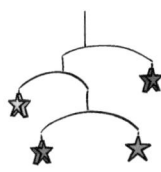

mobile

móvil para bebés

board game

juego de mesa

dice

dados

model train set

tren eléctrico

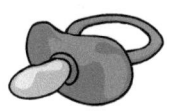

pacifier

maniquí

party

fiesta

picture book

álbum de fotos

ball

balón

doll

muñeca

play

jugar

sandpit

arenero

swing

columpio

toys

juguetes

video game console

consode videojuegos

tricycle

triciclo

teddy bear

oso de peluche

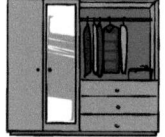

wardrobe

clóset

clothing

ropa

socks

calcetines

stockings

pantimedias

tights

mallas

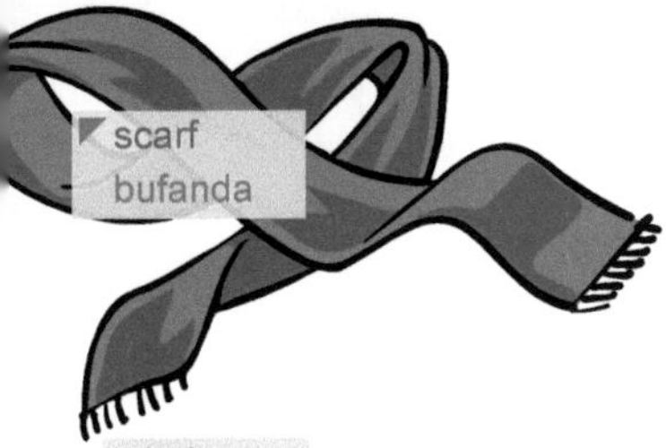

scarf
bufanda

umbrella
paraguas

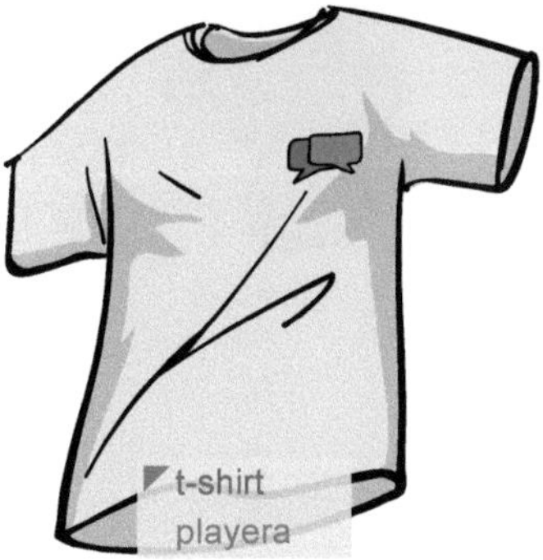

t-shirt
playera

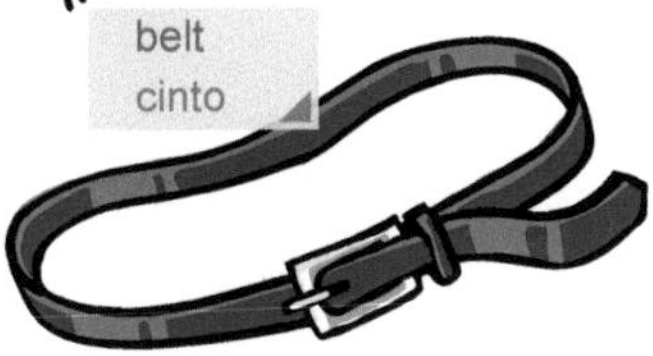

belt
cinto

boots
botas

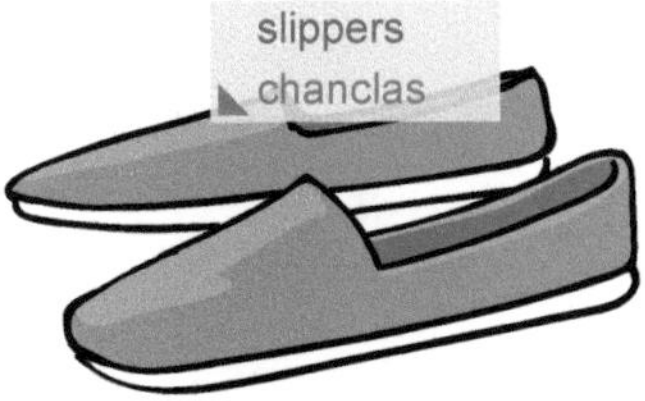

slippers
chanclas

sneakers
tenis

sandals
sandalias

shoes
zapatos

rubber boots
botas de goma

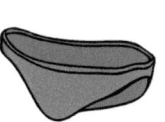

underwear
ropa interior

bra
brasier

undershirt
chaleco

clothing - ropa

body

body

pants

pantalones

jeans

pantalones de mezclilla

skirt

falda

blouse

blusa

shirt

camisa

pullover

suéter

sweater

sudadera

blazer

saco sport

jacket

chamarra

coat

abrigo

raincoat

impermeable

costume

traje

dress

vestido

wedding dress

vestido de novia

suit

traje

nightgown

camisón

pajamas

pijama

sari

sari

headscarf

pañuelo para cabeza

turban

turbante

burka

burka

kaftan

caftán

abaya

abaya

swimsuit

traje de baño

trunks

short de baño

shorts

shorts

tracksuit

pants

apron

delantal

gloves

guantes

button
botón

glasses
gafas

bracelet
brazalete

necklace
collar

ring
anillo

earring
arete

cap
gorra

coat hanger
gancho

hat
sombrero

tie
corbata

zip
cierre

helmet
casco

braces
tirantes

school uniform
uniforme

uniform
uniforme

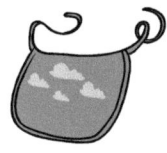

bib

babero

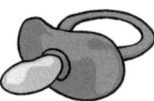

pacifier

maniquí

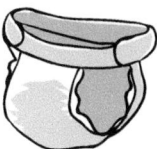

diaper

pañal

office
oficina

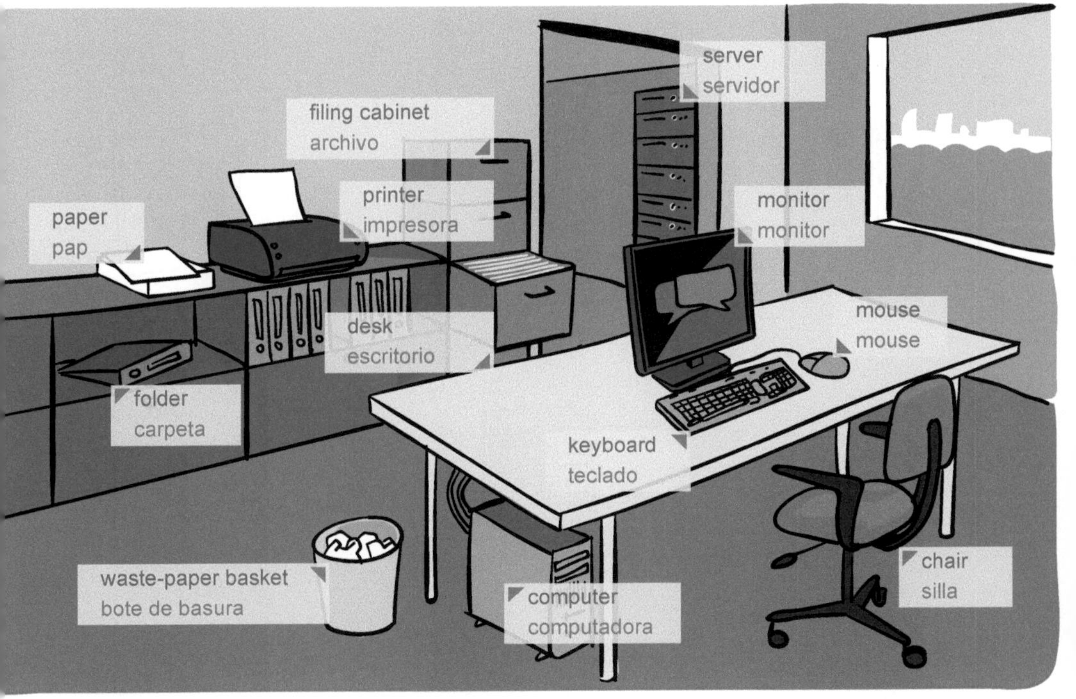

server
servidor
filing cabinet
archivo
printer
impresora
paper
pap
monitor
monitor
mouse
mouse
desk
escritorio
folder
carpeta
keyboard
teclado
waste-paper basket
bote de basura
computer
computadora
chair
silla

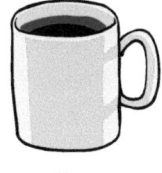

coffee mug

taza de café

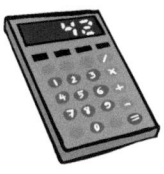

calculator

calculadora

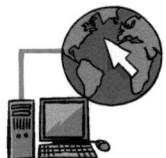

internet

internet

laptop
notebook

letter
carta

message
mensaje

cell phone
móvil

network
red

photocopier
fotocopiadora

software
software

telephone
teléfono

plug socket
tomacorriente

fax machine
fax

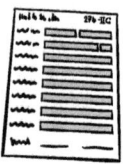

form
formulario

document
documento

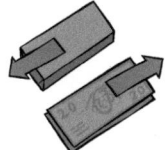

buy

comprar

pay

pagar

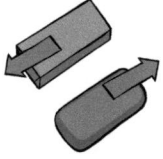

trade

hacer negocios

money

dinero

 USD

dollar

dólar

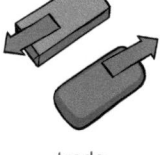 EUR

euro

euro

 JPY

yen

yen

 RUB

rouble

rublo

 CHF

Swiss franc

franco suizo

 CNY

renminbi yuan

yuan

 INR

rupee

rupia

cash point

cajero automático

currency exchange office

casa de cambio

gold

oro

silver

plata

oil

petróleo

energy

energía

price

precio

contract

contrato

tax

impuesto

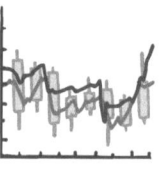

stock

acción

work

trabajar

employee

empleado

employer

empleador

factory

fábrica

shop

tienda

occupations
ocupaciones

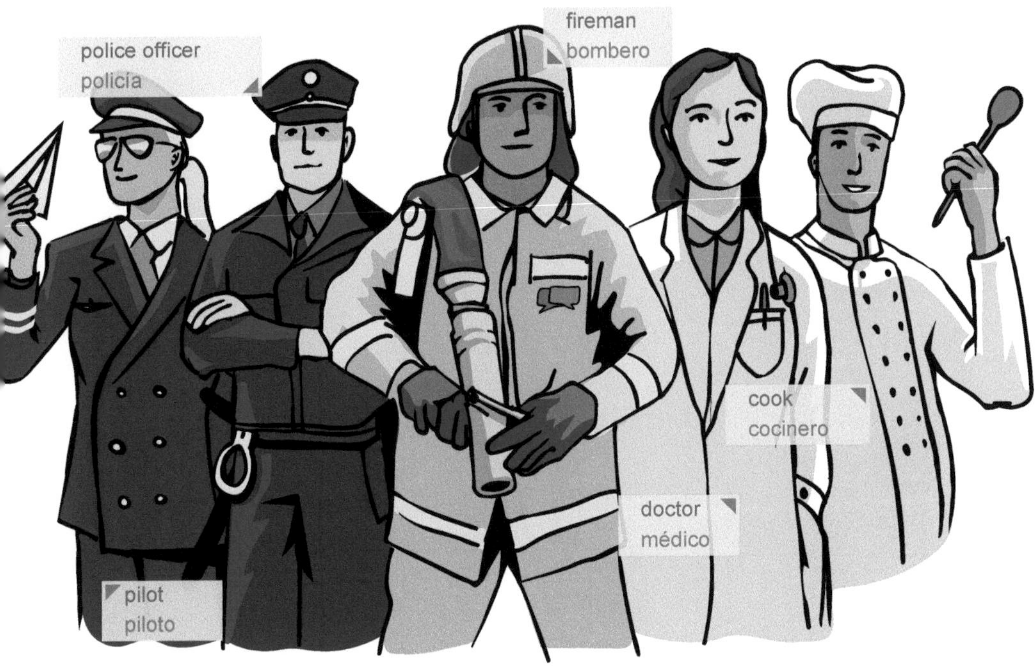
police officer
policía
fireman
bombero
cook
cocinero
doctor
médico
pilot
piloto

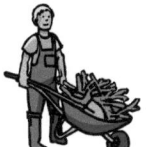

gardener

jardinero

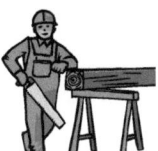

carpenter

carpintero

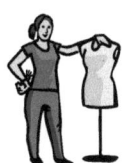

seamstress

costurera

judge

juez

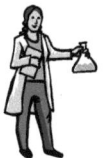

chemist

farmacéutico

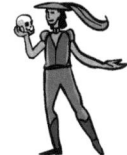

actor

actor

bus driver

conductor de autobús

taxi driver

taxista

fisherman

pescador

cleaning lady

señora de limpieza

roofer

instalador de techos

waiter

camarero

hunter

cazador

painter

pintor

baker

panadero

electrician

electricista

builder

obrero

engineer

ingeniero

butcher

carnicero

plumber

plomero

postman

cartero

soldier

soldado

architect

arquitecto

cashier

cajero

florist

florista

hairdresser

peluquero

conductor

cobrador

mechanic

mecánico

captain

capitán

dentist

dentista

scientist

científico

rabbi

rabino

imam

imán

monk

monje

pastor

sacerdote

tools
herramientas

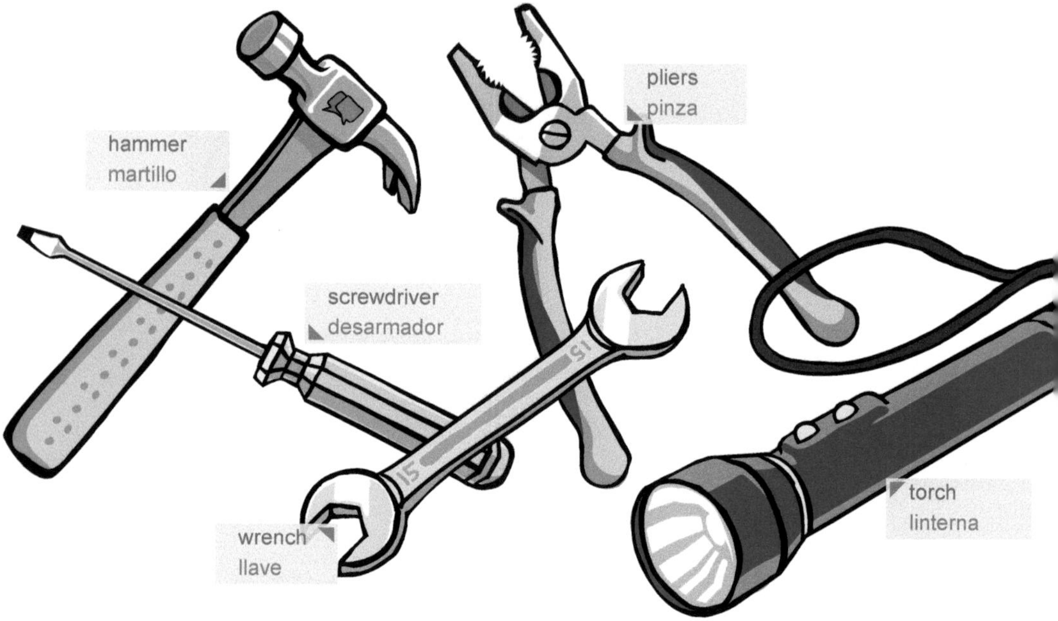
hammer
martillo
pliers
pinza
screwdriver
desarmador
wrench
llave
torch
linterna

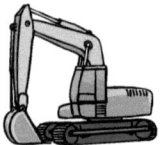

excavator
excavadora

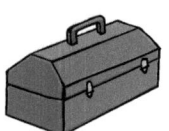

toolbox
caja de herramientas

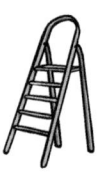

ladder
escalera de mano

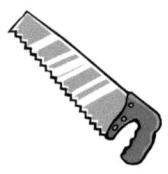

saw
sierra

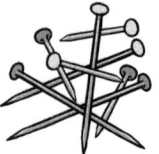

nails
clavos

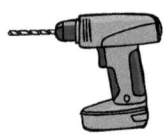

drill
taladro

repair
reparar

shovel
pala

Damn!
¡Maldición!

dustpan
recogedor

paint can
bote de pintura

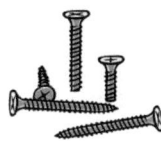

screws
tornillos

musical instruments
instrumentos musicales

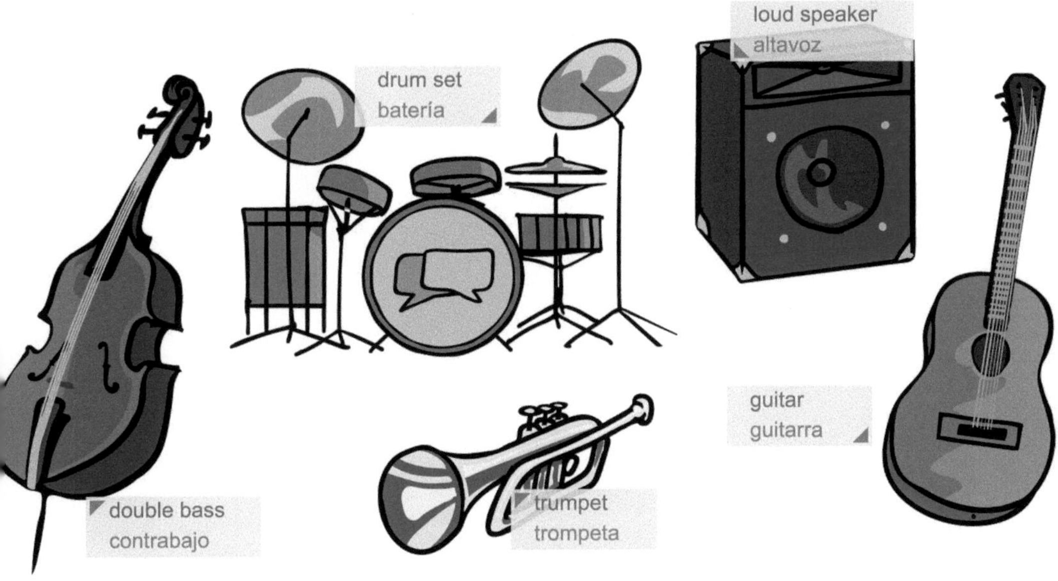

drum set
batería

loud speaker
altavoz

guitar
guitarra

double bass
contrabajo

trumpet
trompeta

piano

piano

violin

violín

bass

bajo

timpani

timbales

drums

tambor

keyboard

teclado

saxophone

saxofón

flute

flauta

microphone

micrófono

musical instruments - instrumentos musicales

zoológico

entrance
entrada

tiger
tigre

cage
jaula

zebra
cebra

animal feed
alimento para animales

panda
oso panda

animals
animales

elephant
elefante

kangaroo
canguro

rhino
rinoceronte

gorilla
gorila

bear
oso

camel

camello

ostrich

avestruz

lion

león

monkey

mono

flamingo

flamenco

parrot

loro

polar bear

oso polar

penguin

pingüino

shark

tiburón

peacock

pavo real

snake

serpiente

crocodile

cocodrilo

zookeeper

guardián de zoológico

seal

foca

jaguar

jaguar

pony
poni

leopard
leopardo

hippo
hipopótamo

giraffe
jirafa

eagle
águila

boar
jabalí

fish
pescado

turtle
tortuga

walrus
morsa

fox
zorro

gazelle
gacela

sports
deportes

American football
fútbol americano

cycling
ciclismo

tennis
tenis

basketball
baloncesto

swimming
natación

boxing
boxeo

ice hockey
hockey sobre hielo

soccer
fútbol

badminton
bádminton

athletics
atletismo

handball
handball

skiing
esquí

polo
polo

jump
saltar

laugh
reír

hug
abrazar

walk
caminar

sing
cantar

dream
soñar

pray
rezar

kiss
besar

write
escribir

draw
dibujar

show
mostrar

push
empujar

give
dar

take
tomar

have
tener

do
hacer

be
ser

stand
estar parado

run
correr

pull
jalar

throw
arrojar

fall
caer

lie
estar acostado

wait
esperar

carry
llevar

sit
estar sentado

get dressed
vestirse

sleep
dormir

wake up
despertar

look at

mirar

cry

llorar

stroke

acariciar

comb

peinar

talk

hablar

understand

entender

ask

preguntar

listen

escuchar

drink

beber

eat

comer

tidy up

ordenar

love

amar

cook

cocinar

drive

conducir

fly

volar

sail

navegar

calculate

calcular

read

leer

learn

aprender

work

trabajar

marry

casarse

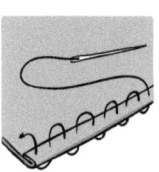

sew

coser

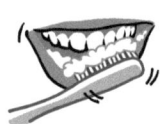

brush teeth

cepillarse los dientes

kill

matar

smoke

fumar

send

enviar

grandmother
abuela

grandfather
abuelo

father
padre

mother
madre

baby
bebé

daughter
hija

son
hijo

guest

invitado

aunt

tía

uncle

tío

brother

hermano

sister

hermana

body

cuerpo

forehead
frente
eye
ojo
shoulder
hombro
finger
dedo
face
cara
chin
barbilla
hand
mano
leg
pierna
breast
pecho
arm
brazo

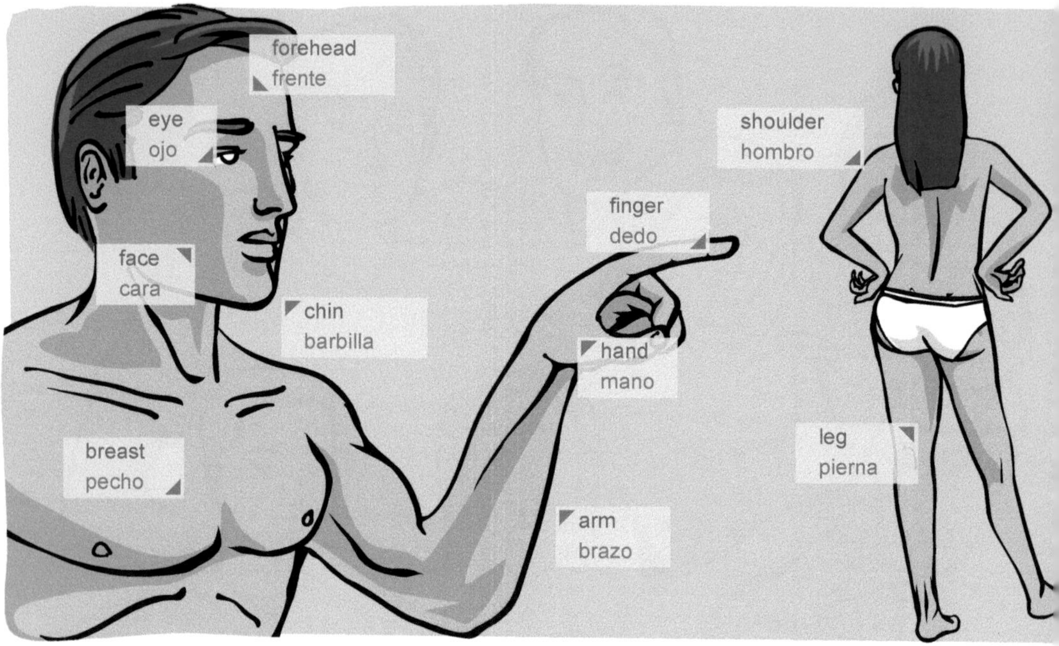

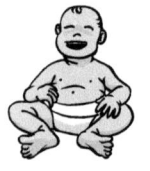

baby

bebé

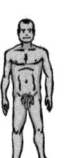

man

hombre

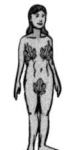

woman

mujer

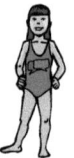

girl

niña

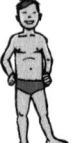

boy

niño

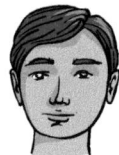

head

cabeza

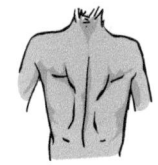

back
....
espalda

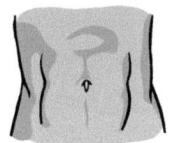

belly
....
barriga

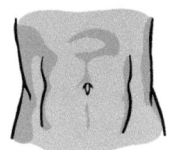

navel
....
ombligo

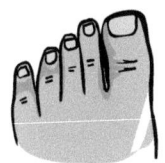

toe
....
dedo dpie

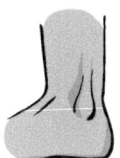

heel
....
talón

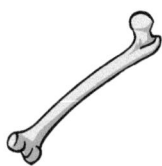

bone
....
hueso

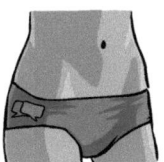

hip
....
cadera

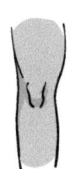

knee
....
rodilla

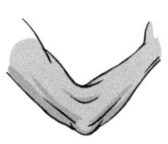

elbow
....
codo

nose
....
nariz

buttocks
....
pompis

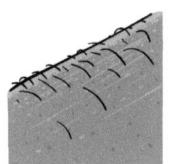

skin
....
piel

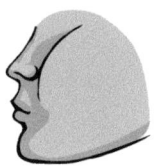

cheek
....
mejilla

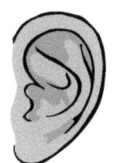

ear
....
oído

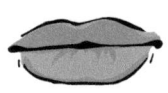

lip
....
labio

body - cuerpo

mouth
boca

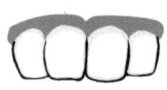

tooth
diente

tongue
lengua

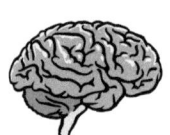

brain
cerebro

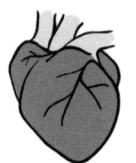

heart
corazón

muscle
músculo

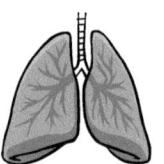

lung
pulmón

liver
hígado

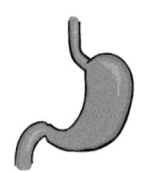

stomach
estómago

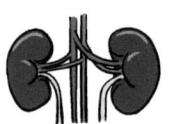

kidneys
riñones

sex
sexo

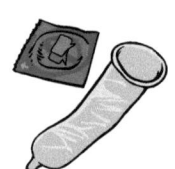

condom
condón

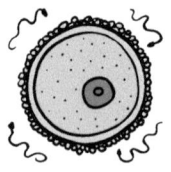

ovum
óvulo

semen
semen

pregnancy
embarazo

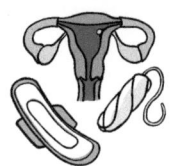

menstruation

menstruación

vagina

vagina

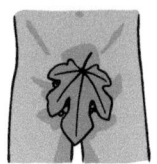

penis

pene

eyebrow

ceja

hair

cabello

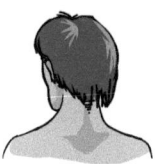

neck

cuello

hospital
hospital

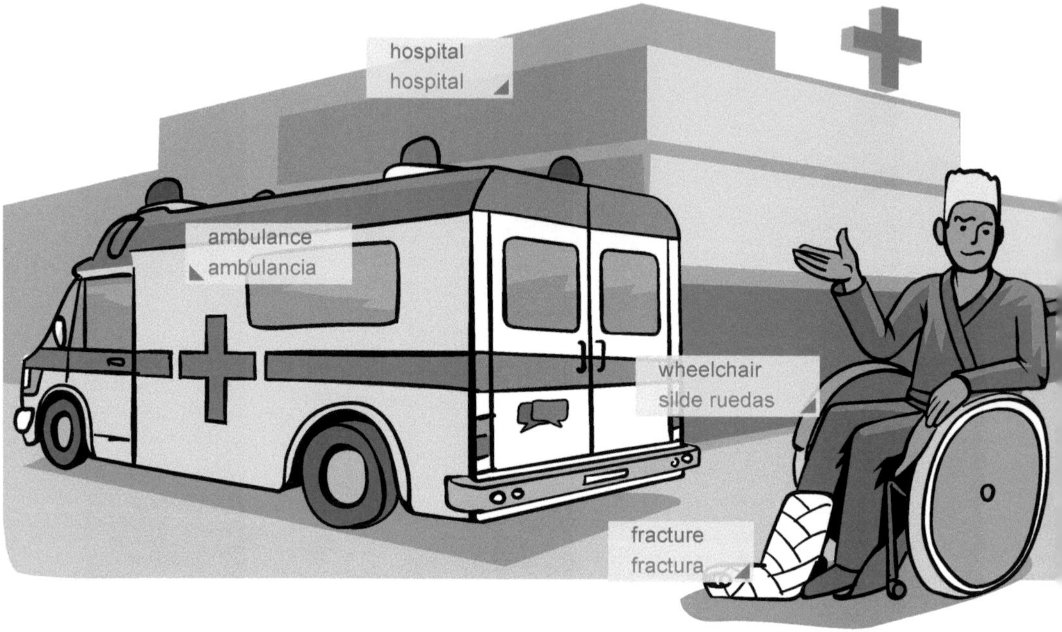

hospital
hospital
ambulance
ambulancia
wheelchair
silde ruedas
fracture
fractura

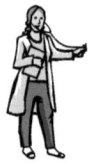

doctor

médico

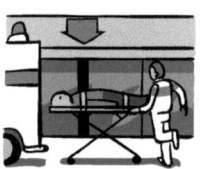

emergency room

sade emergencias

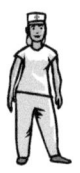

nurse

enfermera

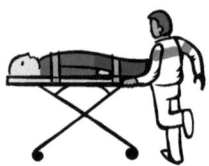

emergency

emergencia

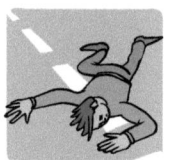

unconscious

inconsciente

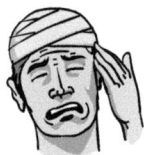

pain

dolor

injury

lesión

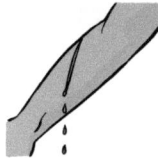

bleeding

hemorragia

heart attack

infarto

stroke

accidente cerebrovascular

allergy

alergia

cough

tos

fever

fiebre

flu

gripa

diarrhea

diarrea

headache

dolor de cabeza

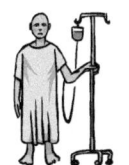

cancer

cáncer

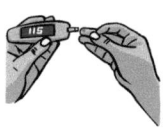

diabetes

diabetes

surgeon

cirujano

scalpel

bisturí

operation

operación

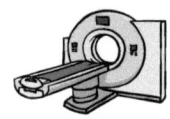

CT
TC

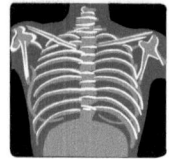

x-ray
rayos x

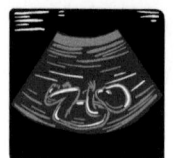

ultrasound
ultrasonido

face mask
mascarilla

disease
enfermedad

waiting room
sade espera

crutch
muleta

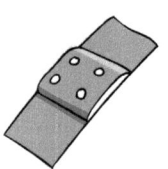

plaster
vendita

bandage
vendaje

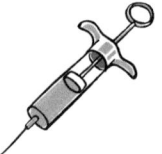

injection
inyección

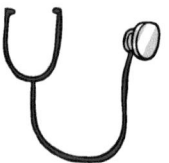

stethoscope
estetoscopio

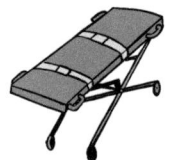

stretcher
camilla

clinical thermometer
termómetro

birth
nacimiento

overweight
sobrepeso

hearing aid

audífono

disinfectant

desinfectante

infection

infección

virus

virus

HIV / AIDS

VIH / SIDA

medicine

medicina

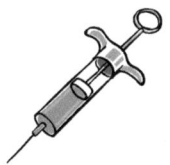

vaccination

vacunación

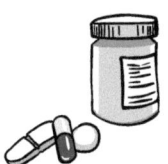

tablets

tabletas

pill

pastilanticonceptiva

emergency call

llamada de emergencia

blood pressure monitor

medidor de presión

ill / healthy

enfermo / sano

Help!

¡Socorro!

alarm

alarma

assault

agresión

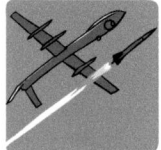

attack

ataque

danger

peligro

emergency exit

salida de emergencia

Fire!

¡Fuego!

fire extinguisher

extintor de incendios

accident

accidente

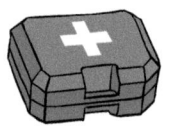

first-aid kit

botiquín de primeros
auxilios

SOS

SOS

police

policía

Europe

Europa

North America

Norteamérica

South America

Sudamérica

Africa

África

Asia

Asia

Australia

Australia

Atlantic

Atlántico

Pacific

Pacífico

Indian Ocean

Océano Índico

Antarctic Ocean

Océano Antártico

Arctic Ocean

Océano Ártico

North pole

polo norte

South pole

polo sur

Antarctica

Antártida

earth

tierra

land

tierra

sea

mar

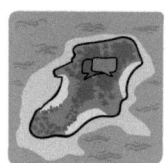

island

isla

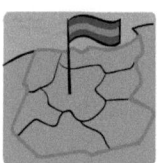

nation

nación

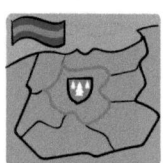

state

estado

clock face
....
esfera

hour hand
....
manecilde las horas

minute hand
....
minutero

second hand
....
segundero

What time is it?
....
¿Qué hora es?

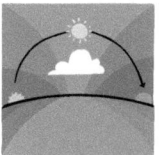

day
....
día

time
....
hora

now
....
ahora

digital watch
....
reloj digital

minute
....
minuto

hour
....
hora

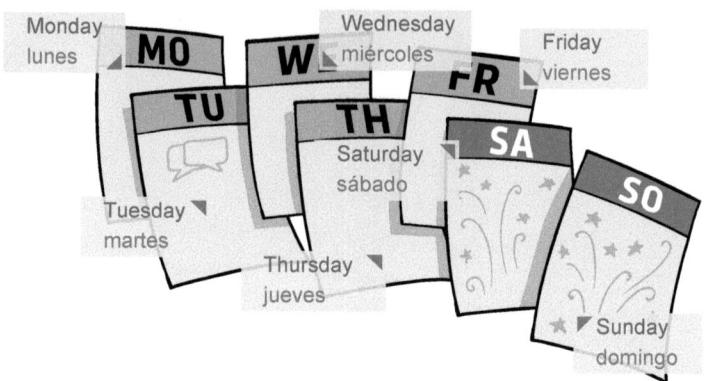

Monday
lunes

Wednesday
miércoles

Friday
viernes

Tuesday
martes

Saturday
sábado

Thursday
jueves

Sunday
domingo

yesterday

ayer

today

hoy

tomorrow

mañana

morning

mañana

noon

mediodía

evening

tarde

MO	TU	WE	TH	FR	SA	SU
1	2	3	4	5	6	7
8	9	10	11	12	13	14
15	16	17	18	19	20	21
22	23	24	25	26	27	28
29	30	31	1	2	3	4

workdays

días laborables

MO	TU	WE	TH	FR	SA	SU
1	2	3	4	5	6	7
8	9	10	11	12	13	14
15	16	17	18	19	20	21
22	23	24	25	26	27	28
29	30	31	1	2	3	4

weekend

fin de semana

year

año

rain
lluvia
rainbow
arco iris
wind
viento
snow
nieve
spring
primavera
summer
verano
fall
otoño
winter
invierno

4.APRIL 11°
5.APRIL 4°
6.APRIL 13°
7.APRIL 8°
8.APRIL 10°

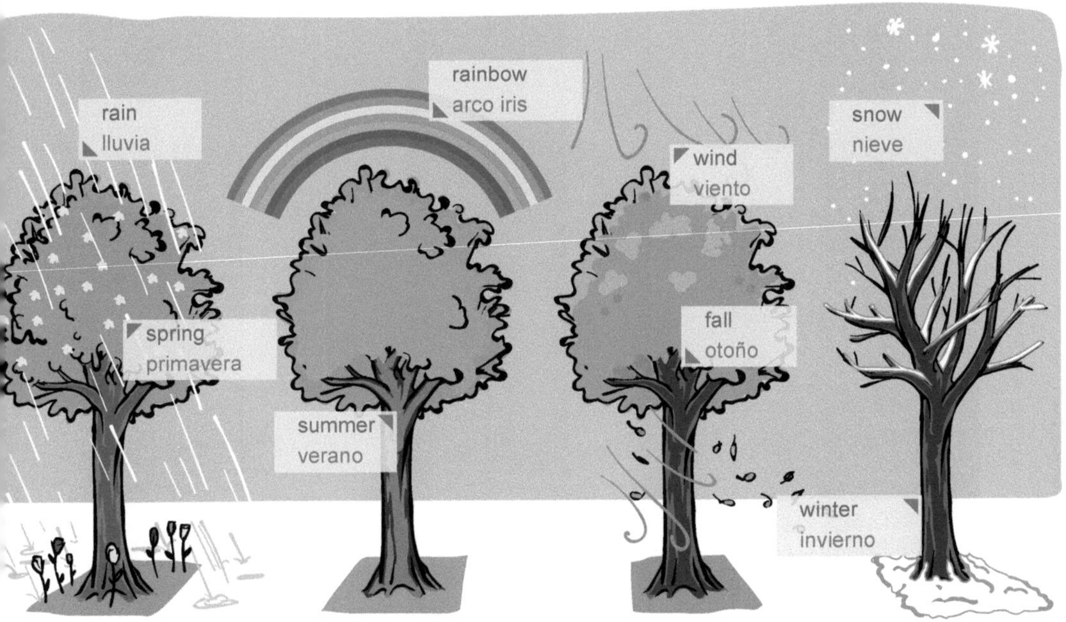

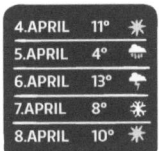

weather forecast

pronóstico dtiempo

F C
120 40
90 30
60 20
30 10
0 0
-30 -10
-20

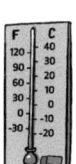

thermometer

termómetro

sunshine

sol

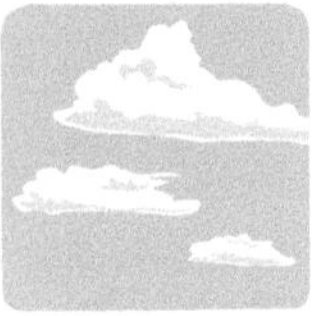

cloud

nube

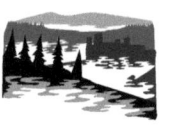

fog

niebla

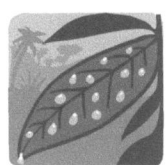

humidity

humedad

lightning

rayo

thunder

trueno

storm

tormenta

hail

granizo

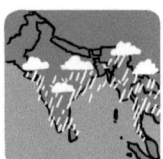

monsoon

monzón

flood

inundación

ice

hielo

January

enero

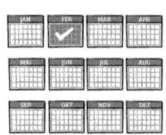

February

febrero

March

marzo

April

abril

May

mayo

June

junio

July

julio

August

agosto

September
....
septiembre

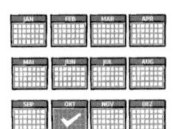

October
....
octubre

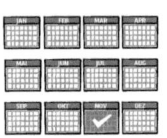

November
....
noviembre

December
....
diciembre

circle
....
círculo

square
....
cuadrado

rectangle
....
rectángulo

triangle
....
triángulo

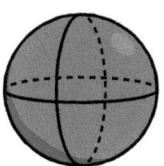

sphere
....
esfera

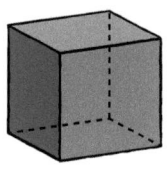

cube
....
cubo

colors

colores

white

blanco

yellow

amarillo

orange

naranja

pink

rosa

red

rojo

purple

morado

blue

azul

green

verde

brown

marrón

gray

gris

black

negro

a lot / a little

mucho / poco

angry / calm

enojado / tranquilo

beautiful / ugly

bonito / feo

beginning / end

principio / fin

big / small

grande / pequeño

bright / dark

claro / oscuro

brother / sister

hermano / hermana

clean / dirty

limpio / sucio

complete / incomplete

completo / incompleto

day / night

día / noche

dead / alive

muerto / vivo

wide / narrow

ancho / angosto

edible / inedible

comestible / no comestible

evil / kind

malo / amable

excited / bored

entusiasmado / aburrido

fat / thin

gordo / delgado

first / last

primero / último

friend / enemy

amigo / enemigo

full / empty

lleno / vacío

hard / soft

duro / blando

heavy / light

pesado / ligero

hunger / thirst

hambre / sed

ill / healthy

enfermo / sano

illegal / legal

ilegal / legal

intelligent / stupid

inteligente / tonto

left / right

izquierda / derecha

near / far

cerca / lejos

new / used
nuevo / usado

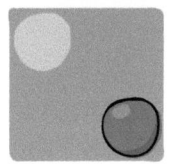

nothing / something
nada / algo

old / young
viejo / joven

on / off
encendido / apagado

open / closed
abierto / cerrado

quiet / loud
silencioso / ruidoso

rich / poor
rico / pobre

right / wrong
correcto / incorrecto

rough / smooth
áspero / suave

sad / happy
triste / contento

short / long
corto / largo

slow / fast
lento / rápido

wet / dry
húmedo / seco

warm / cool
caliente / frío

war / peace
guerra / paz

0

zero
cero

1

one
uno

2

two
dos

3

three
tres

4

four
cuatro

5

five
cinco

6

six
seis

7

seven
siete

8

eight
ocho

9

nine
nueve

10

ten
diez

11

eleven
once

12

twelve

doce

13

thirteen

trece

14

fourteen

catorce

15

fifteen

quince

16

sixteen

dieciséis

17

seventeen

diecisiete

18

eighteen

dieciocho

19

nineteen

diecinueve

20

twenty

veinte

100

hundred

cien

1.000

thousand

mil

1.000.000

million

millón

numbers - números

English

inglés

American English

inglés americano

Chinese Mandarin

chino mandarín

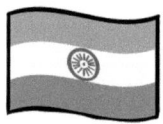

Hindi

hindi

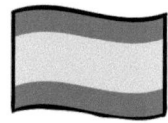

Spanish

español

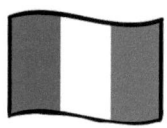

French

francés

Arabic

árabe

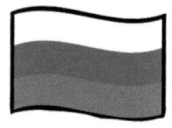

Russian

ruso

Portuguese

portugués

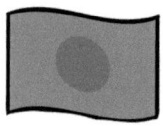

Bengali

bengalí

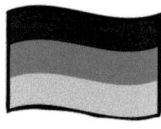

German

alemán

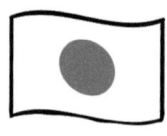

Japanese

japonés

I
yo

you
tú

he / she / it
él / ella

we
nosotros

you
vosotros

they
ellos

who?
¿quién?

what?
¿qué?

how?
¿cómo?

where?
¿dónde?

when?
¿cuándo?

name
nombre

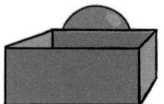

behind

detrás

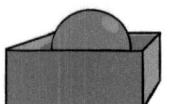

in

en

in front of

delante de

over

por encima de

on

sobre

under

debajo de

beside

junto a

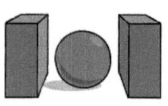

between

entre

place

lugar